Wicked Women

Wicked Women

Leslie Simon

RESOURCE *Publications* · Eugene, Oregon

WICKED WOMEN

Resource Publications
An Imprint of Wipf and Stock Publishers
199 W. 8th Ave., Suite 3
Eugene, OR 97401

www.wipfandstock.com

PAPERBACK ISBN: 979-8-3852-3696-1
HARDCOVER ISBN: 979-8-3852-3697-8
EBOOK ISBN: 979-8-3852-3698-5

VERSION NUMBER 02/03/25

To Mr. Sabel who told me I had a poet's heart
&
Ms. Lacy who reminded me to follow it

"In a world where men are the monster-makers, what makes women evil?"

Acknowledgments

This book would be a collection of half-written poems, scribbled notes, and dog-eared textbook pages without the support of my family, a slew of sage mentors, and the Wipf and Stock Publishing team. Thank you:

To Matt Wimer, who took a chance on a handful of imperfect poems and the idea that even the wickedest women deserve to be heard, and to the team at Wipf and Stock, who made me feel at ease with the unfamiliar world of publishing.

To Justin Somper, author of *Vampirates*, for inspiring eight-year-old me to love the outcasts, and for answering all my pressing literary questions about writing, editing, character, and everything in between.

To Stephanie Lacy for finding something lovable in the ugliness of every rough draft, dud, and half-fleshed out idea, and for reminding me to tell the stories I want to tell.

To Dan Sabel and Lisa Watrous for rekindling my love of writing. Sometimes being told, "You are an author," is all it takes to convince you, you are.

To my father, who first opened my eyes to the power of storytelling with his deliciously silly tales of adventure, and my mother, who reminded me illustrations do not have to be perfect to be impactful (the same is true of authors).

To Gigi for a name worth stamping on a book cover. To Carissa for keeping me grounded and Esgar for being a sound shoulder and safe space, but most of all for being a friend.

To my sisters, who remind me every day how badass and beautiful women can be.

And finally, to God. He gave me the words, the idea, and the voice to bring these women's stories to life. For that I am forever grateful.

Bonnie Parker:
The Outlaw Poet

I'm going to be on movie screens
I'm going to be a star
I'm going to steal the starlets' scenes
Clyde swears it on his car

I watch the moving picture shows
And dream it will be me
From my hand a poem flows
Unbidden, bright, and free

With every day I grow more sure
My love will get me far
Clyde's music is a soul-stitch cure
For scrape, and hurt, and scar

He missteps oft, that's God's good truth
But we all stink of sin
A tragedy of foolish youth
Where poverty steals wins

My poems are prophetic doom
But Clyde can't see ahead
I know our deaths creep near and loom
Will Ma cry when I'm dead?

The cops will cower out of sight
As death breathes down our necks
Without a chance to scream or fight
Our bodies will be wrecks

I'll gasp, and stare, and hand in hand
I'll think of Ma at home
Of how cops had our whole fall planned
As if we were like Rome

It makes me sad, I'm who I am
An outlaw set on stars
A beauty queen stuck on the lam
A gun moll with cigars

Textbooks always paint me mean
A temptress with a tongue
Such pictures are a touch obscene
My crime was being young

They buried me away from Clyde
In different plots of ground
My ghost still lingers at his side
Together we are found

And silver screens that I adored
Now tell my tale each night
And I delight to hear I'm still
A princess to Clyde's knight

The Outlaw Poet

Nellie Madison:
California's Death Row Dame

It's not my fault I shot him up
My man was crude and cruel
He treated me like I was trash
He took me for a fool

He threw a knife and I struck back
He should have watched hisself
I was not made for lying flat
For sitting on a shelf

I planned his death, I took great care
I did the deed real quick
I argued it was self-defense
The jury thought me thick

They sentenced me to die alone
To flake and waste away
I begged the state to stay the noose
To keep my end at bay

When all was said, I served my time
I held my head up high
I fell in love with someone kind
Who never made me cry

I lived my days out fast and rough
And then I said goodbye
I can't say I regret it much
You love, you kill, you die

Ruth Judd:
The Trunk Murderess

A man can drive a woman mad
When he strings a girl along
And sings a perfect song of love
And pretends he does no wrong

And when he sets his eyes on Ann
And flirts with Sammy too
There's little else to say or think
You know just what to do

You wait until the evening falls
And creep into their home
Your friends are safe and sleeping sound
And so you're free to roam

You step real soft, your footsteps light
But guns are bloody loud
Sammy wakes and screams in fear
You shoot and drape a shroud

What to do? you start to think
These bodies can't stay here
You go to work and filch a trunk
To make them disappear

You cut them up in small, neat chunks
Then shove them deep inside
You ship the trunks to Tinseltown
And follow for the ride

But cases full of bodies smell
Of foul and wrongful deaths
And you get caught mighty quick
Your hands are Ms. Macbeth's

The trial draws a record crowd
You cause a raucous scene
And when they sentence you to life
You act right mad and mean

A looney bin is where it's at
That's where you ought to be
But once you're locked behind steel doors
You pack your bag and flee

You bite your tongue and take a job
Where wages go unpaid
So you decide to go to court
And there your fortune's made

You live until you're lined and old
Alone, aloof, and tame
And when they ask about the trunk
You always shift the blame

"It's not my fault they stepped to me
They took that man of mine
And now they rot for what they did
I think that's just divine"

Elizabeth Báthory:
The Blood Countess

I hear the gossip of the swine
I know they think I'm mad
I cannot help but hurt what's mine
My empathy's gone bad

I whip, and maim, and bleed girls low
I bathe in blood and screams
I make their endings foul and slow
And shred them at the seams

Their fathers think me fang and wings
A demon sent from hell
I lick their blood from lips and rings
And sing a soft farewell

They never think that it's a lie
This cutout in a crown
No, I'm a witch with evil eye
A girl they'd like to drown

A tale as old as Eden is
They paint us girls as snakes
And crucify us for their bliss
With rumors that are fakes

But in the end I do not die
A myth in blood they wrought
A demon who can sail the sky
Whose youth is dire bought

There's little worse for girls to be
Than feared beyond all sense
I wonder what they'd think of me
Without the dark suspense

Would they hate me even still
For daring to stand tall
Or would they always wish me ill
Because I did not fall

Such questions do not soothe my soul
The damage has been done
But I believe it's good to know
The lies that men have spun

The Blood Countess

Lizzie Borden:
Axe Murderer

Lizzie Borden took an axe
And cut her Ma to bits
She kicked her with her leather toe
And gored her brain to grits

Father dozing on the couch
Was woke with fatal fate
To chop his head was bloody fun
She dropped the blade in hate

This is what they say of me
Despite my guilt-free trial
They think I am a wicked witch
They say that I am vile

I did not kill my Ma, God's truth
I did not hate my Pa
I might have wished they both were dead
But never broke the law

They could not prove I did the crime
My clothes were lost and charred
But after all they heard of me
I suffered foul regard

They hated me, I see that now
I had no means or beau
But I was just a spinster pure
Against the status quo

A boring girl without a tale
I should have lived and died
But papers made me what I'm not
They only told one side

So, I suppose it does some good
To tell you how it was
But I suspect you'll hate me still
Your reason, "Just because"

I was not loved, I was maligned
Townspeople dubbed me odd
'Cause I was plain and dowdy true
A woman feared of God

My father was a thrifty bloke
He held his purse tight closed
My Step Ma was a mean old twat
I'm glad she was deposed

My sister Emma loved me dear
She was my ray of light
And Alice was my confidante
Her future shone quite bright

Foul rumors cast their filth on them
The papers smeared their names
But they were just the sweetest girls
A righteous pair of dames

I don't know how my parents died
The scene was gruesome bad
I think it was a stranger with
A temper I might add

But in the end, it matters not
I'm far more fun to blame
And I delight in being known
By picture and by name

But please do not despise of me
What others claim I did
I was no perfect daughter
But I was no evil kid

Belle Starr:
The Bandit Queen

Sitting on a saddled horse
Laced in velvet black
Holding double guns aloft
Poised for the attack

I ran with outlaws mean as pitch
I robbed horsekeepers blind
I smiled like a hangman's noose
I never was called kind

I wed a man with amber skin
He loved me as his bride
And then he died a tragic death
And on his grave I cried

An outlaw queen without her king
A bride without her groom
And everywhere I dared to ride
Grief was in fresh bloom

I danced a jig with men I found
To try and patch the pain
But as I left, I spun and found
A bullet in my brain

Beside a creek they left me there
To wither on the vine
Shooting me until I croaked
Until the dirt was wine

They never solved who murdered me
They let him win the day
And so I haunt that sorry sand
Where once my body lay

Mary Ann Cotton:
The Black Widow

A little poison in their wine
A little in their bread
Arsenic with their morning meal
A sprinkle till they're dead

A husband and some bonny babes
What good are they to me?
For I cannot afford to live
On cabbage leaves and tea

No, I would sooner kill them
Their murders pay the bills
And decorate myself in lace
In diamond rings and frills

They couldn't catch me for them all
But caught me for the one
I guess they thought me cursed real good
For murdering my son

The noose did sway from side to side
I kept my eyes upshot
For I would sooner die a queen
Than likely die as not

I said a prayer and crossed my heart
I tried to be a saint
I cannot help I hurt them so
My soul was the complaint

I rot in hell like I deserve
Though really, it's unfair
For evidence they never had
Just theories they declared

The Black Widow

Catherine de' Medici:
The Black Queen

She is me, that banker queen
Pure blood of Florence fair
Whose greatest crime was lashing out
When men would stare or glare

I'm often blamed by history
For maiming Huguenots
But what was I to do, my dears?
I did not shoot those shots

All I did was angle for
My sons to reign supreme
And any Ma would do the same
No matter the extreme

Because of me the Valois name
Is known as something grand
Without my hand it'd be for naught
They'd have no leg to stand

Like every queen I'm called a witch
Who hid behind her sons
I'd rather "witch" than be the one
Who fled from swords and guns

So, hate me if you really must
My soul can rest at ease
I am not the villain and
Ambition's no disease

Leonarda Cianciulli:
The Soap Maker of Correggio

"In your hand asylum waits
In your head's a prison"
The fortune teller dictates fates
Like Christ before he's risen

I pick her brain for greater truth
And she reveals my curse
I'll lose my children in their youth
Their cribs will be their hearse

And sure enough, just like she reads
I lose each little lamb
I plant them in the earth like seeds
A mourning Ma, I am

All thirteen babes they die and go
Excepting four strong tykes
And I become the hate I sow
I dream of blades and spikes

And so, I hatch a wicked plot
My first kill's easy prey
I throw her bits into the pot
And watch her melt away

Just a pinch of powdered paste
I purchased to make soap
I'd hate to let her go to waste
Her death fills me with hope

A tick of time, she's just the fat
I pour her from the pot
A globby mess that slops and splats
Right down the drainage slot

I take her leavings on the stove
And make them into cakes
I feed them to my darling drove
And spoon them to the snakes

I should have stopped right then and there
But I was mad and ill
I thought if I killed someone rare
I'd spare my son death's chill

Two more women smeared the stone
Before my bloody blade
And I consumed them to the bone
In sweet treats that I made

I was not crazy, can't you see
I only wanted peace
To someday set my children free
And make my grieving cease

If you would damn a Ma for that
Then maybe you're the cur
For I would rather chew the fat
Then suffer things that were

Anne Bonny & Mary Read:
The Pirate Queens

Across the seven seas we sailed
With venom on our tongues
And hair that hung in flowing waves
With fire in our lungs

We gave as good as any man
We filched and stole and fought
But in the end our Rackham fell
The both of we was caught

We hissed and spat till blue and broke
We did not give up fast
We held our ground as best we could
Until the very last

And when we saw that we was beat
We did not tuck our tails
We held our heads up high and proud
And glanced up at the sails

The dogs below were dragged up top
They wobbled on their feet
While we did fight, they drunk their fill
And caused our last retreat

Cut and bruised we seethed with hate
We clenched our teeth and spat
"While you were out fast sleeping
Us girls were at the bat"

They locked us in a cellar
Stuffed full of mold and rats
And pointed at the bones they left
"We fed their flesh to cats"

Set to hang and die as scum
We hatched a plot real smart
For we were both with child then
I told them from the heart

"You can't kill us, you'll kill the babes
We really must not hang
But if you want to kill us still
Please wait till they have sprang"

And so, we stewed for nine long months
Alone with just the cries
Of all the dogs who brought us there
And all the corpsy flies

A prison cell is not the place
To birth a babe so small
But still we held those wailing sprouts
Our greatest treasure haul

And as we nursed those tiny tykes
Jack Rackham he did swing
And we rejoiced to see the snow
Start thawing into spring

They let us free and told us plain
"You better stay real clean"
We crossed our hearts and sleeping babes
"That's the last we'll both be seen"

The Pirate Queens

Beverley Allitt: The Angel of Death

I know that I'm a danger
To myself and infant dears
But when I see them sleeping
I can't control my fears

I lift those darlings in my arms
I rock them till they snore
And as they doze I draw the dose
A murder minus gore

They slip away in little spurts
With tears I watch them go
I know they'll be far safer
Once their bodies sleep below

Some people call it evil
But I think it's rather smart
To save them from the hurting
Before the hurting starts

And why should all those foolish girls
Have babies anyways
When I can never have one soul
That fights and breathes and stays

I think my way is better
It's a mercy not to feel
And hopefully God cuts me
A lucky kind of deal

For I deserve a happy end
I've tired of this mess
But I believe I'll suffer still
I know I'm owed far less

No one will ever say of me
"That girl was wicked smart
She kept her head screwed on real straight
She nursed a golden heart"

Instead, they'll say that I was bad
A reaper with no soul
But how can I explain to them
My heart was just a hole

So, though I know it's foolish hope
Remember me polite
For I know you think me evil
But I think I did what's right

Belle Gunness:
Hell's Belle

I died a hero in the flames
Protecting my wee lambs
But when they shook the rubble free
They unearthed my many scams

It came to light I killed a lot
Of wandering lost souls
And chopped off all their body parts
And shoved them into holes

I cashed out on their dusty bones
On husbands, lovers, kids
But never was I ever caught
For what our God forbids

After death they plowed my land
Uncovering old graves
Of every missing person that
I fed to hell's red waves

They marred my name in every print
A woman foolish mad
Who never loved a living soul
Who hated her own lads

And I'd be lying if I said
They did not print the truth
They painted me just as I lived
Just as I was in youth

The greatest bloody murderer
Womanhood produced
A horrid plague of awfulness
Humanity induced

And don't it warm the heart to know
That every patch of land
Might be hiding crimes like mine
On which you likely stand

So everywhere you ever step
I follow at your heel
A plague upon the living lost
A scourge that never heals

Maria Hallett:
The Witch of Wellfleet

I fell in love with Bellamy
The textbooks call him Sam
He sailed across the oceans vast
A pirate on the lam

But once he was my lover dear
A darling sailor boy
A prince of pirates far and near
Of all in his employ

He made a fortune robbing ships
To one day set me free
But oceans are quite wily beasts
He could not tame the sea

Just like Teach and Vane and Kidd
My Black Sam he did fall
And I was left alone and damned
No knowledge of his haul

The townsfolk labeled me a witch
A pirate's widowed bride
But I was not a scheming crone
Those wagging tongues did lie

If I had known his buried gold
Was somewhere lost at sea
I would have made a run for it
And searched through the debris

Alas, I knew naught of his gold
But still I held his heart
And all the gossip papers cried
To tear my limbs apart

And all because I loved a boy
Who left me with the tide
To waltz with Jack Tar in the depths
Of waters where he died

They came for me one lonesome night
Before the gleaming dawn
They hauled me to a hangman's tree
To string up as a pawn

But I was not the witch they claimed
No, I was something worse
And so, I blinked my bleary eyes
And slapped them with a curse

"To all who labeled me a witch
And shipped my Sam to sea
I hope you die a grizzly death
And God ignores your plea

And as you stare into your grave
Choose whichever lie you please
Remember that I told you first
Your care is a disease

For you care not for Sam or me
You hunger for his gold
But I have worked my spell on you
His gold you'll never hold"

The ladder lurched, my feet did kick
My vision it went black
But I would do it all again
To win my Sammy back

And still that sleepy town does talk
Of Bellamy's dark fleet
And of the curse I spit at them
Damn the Witch of Wellfleet!

The Witch of Wellfleet

Dorothea Puente:
The Death House Landlady

They thought me frail and trusted me
To care for sick and poor
But I was not the sweet old gran
They met beside the door

I dressed just like the elderly
I did it with great style
But underneath I plotted death
I killed them with a smile

I needed money sure and plain
I cashed out on their bones
And buried them behind the house
And covered them with stones

The ruse went well until the end
But then it fell apart
I could not make those sheriff lads
Believe I had a heart

They wised up to my scheme real fast
They dragged me out in chains
Past the torn-up carpet heap
And all those bloody stains

They sentenced me to life in jail
I did not bat an eye
Those sickly folks deserved their ends
The best they did was die

Squeaky Fromme: Manson's Little Miss

I cannot say how I became
A fly inside his web
Manson was a charming bloke
I slipped into his ebb

He asked if I was cast away
A loner lost and dazed
I answered him with quite a grin
He shrugged as if unfazed

I followed him from town to town
A little dog at heel
And then one day I got a plan
To help the earth to heal

I bought myself a .45
And ventured to the park
Planning to meet Gerald Ford
To make him hear my bark

I aimed the gun right at his head
His service tackled me
"I didn't shoot," I yelled at them
They would not leave me be

They dragged me off to die in jail
But not before a trial
When Keyes said I was full of hate
I threw him my denial

33

The apple struck him in the face
And garnered me a frown
As I delighted at his pain
My lawyer pinned me down

They locked me up as you'd expect
I tried once to escape
They caught me quick and brought me back
My lungs were out of shape

Eventually I made parole
And now I'm doing fine
But still I love that Charlie boy
That lunatic was mine

Marie Antoinette:
Madame Deficit

They slurred me in the paper
Said obscenities and shames
They called me every slander
Every manner of crude name

They hated me right from the start
A rich girl spoiled sick
But I did not put stock in lies
I did not care a lick

I should have seen the turning tide
I wanted to have fun
But when they set their hate on me
It blotted out the sun

The things they did were cruel and mean
They butchered my best girls
And when I hung my head in shame
I clutched my bloody pearls

They hauled me to the court that day
And painted me a witch
But I would die a fearsome queen
Than tuck-tail as a bitch

I did not give their slurs my time
I did not raise my voice
And when I said they got it wrong
I watched the court rejoice

They did not care that I was dead
In all the ways that count
They hungered for my head to pike
To settle their account

And so, I dressed in black stiff clothes
And glared up at the blade
And as they set my head to chop
I did what I was bade

My head came clean without a fuss
My ladies at my side
They bundled my numb body off
To save my broken pride

And so, they think that I'm a wretch
A leech of olden time
But I was just a lonely queen
Naivety my crime

Madame Deficit

Delilah:
The Seductress of Samson

The Bible paints me as a slut
A beast with liar's tongue
But I was just a luckless girl
A foolish lover, young

A haircut's not a daring deed
But somehow, it's a sin
And once I took his strength from him
His weakness did him in

How am I the one to blame
And not the shallow man
Who could not live without his strength
Without his doting fans?

I loved my Samson, loved him well
But I refused to be
Another voiceless lover girl
Adrift within his sea

So, when I left, I left him broke
For he did not break me
And I would sheer his locks from him
To make his blind eyes see

That I was no mere wilting bud
No dandelion flower
I was raised on female wrath
I lusted after power

I handed him to Philistines
And pocketed their gold
Samson's hurt still haunts my dreams
I wake up feeling cold

If I had known the weight I'd feel
At turning on his trust
I'd have made that poor man kneel
And ground his bones to dust

Maybe then I'd find some peace
In taking back my voice
Maybe then the doubt would cease
I missed some other choice

It is not fair, I tell you now
Us women have to choose
To be the one to make men bow
Or hang inside a noose

I made my choice with little guilt
The smallest brush of frown
For all the blood my Samson spilt
I earned his crooked crown

Mary Tudor:
Bloody Mary

A bloody cur they labeled me
For clinging to the old
But I was born to be a queen
My brother loathed my hold

A woman cannot wear a crown
She's mad and rash and foul
For burning wretches at the stake
She smiles as they howl

But what is wrong with iron fists
With reigning like the men
For wanting to be known as fierce
For wielding wit and pen

I wonder what they'd say of me
If I was just a man
Would they hate me all the same
Or would they be my clan

My father was a gruesome thug
Best known for killing wives
But he's remembered rather fond
Despite their ruined lives

I guess that is the secret rub
To lead you must be male
Or else they'll always think of you
Like moths that must be nailed

A wicked woman I was known
But I was just a girl
And from the grave I raise my voice
My banner I unfurl

Slander me like all the rest
Say my name three times
I will haunt you from the dark
With poetry that rhymes

And as I sneer, you'll start to fret
That all those tales were true
That I was what they said of me
That maybe I'm like you

Rusla:
The Red Woman

My brother was a reigning king
Till Omund claimed his throne
And I went on the warpath with
A burning in my bones

Stikla followed at my side as
Oceans we traversed
Ravaging the Denmark coast
With rage we spat and cursed

Burning down each sleeping town
With nary a regret
Tearing limbs from off the captured
Pirates that we met

A warrior maiden of Norse blood
A killer with red hair
A flaming torch in bloody fields
For enemies to 'ware

Tesandus turned from me in fear
And sided with the Danes
My brother dear who lost his throne
For which I took such pains

I gave up my humanity
Became a monster maid
Stikla too who followed me from
Hearth to blazing raid

I should have kept my anger cool
I should have stayed my hand
But I was mad at what he did
And so I took a stand

I sunk his ship and made him kneel
I could have gored my blade
Instead I let my brother live
But for my heart I paid

His crew, they turned their hate on me
And hunted me for fun
They seized my braids and beat me black
They cheered as it was done

With oars they struck me in the face
My teeth did crack and break
And as I fell in pools of blood
A legend they did make

No one tells Tesandus's tale
They know Rusla the Red
The mighty maid who conquered shores
And never ran nor fled

And Stikla, darling sister dear
She never bowed her head
She fought beside me tooth and claw
Until my blood was shed

And even then, she held me close
And swearing on the skies
She never let those foolish Danes
Forget my final cries

Stikla swore she'd make me known
The fierce and free redhead
She vowed to make the world recall
What Danes had kept for dead

And though I know the world prefers
To talk of Anne and Read
Sweet Stikla and dear Rusla
Were first to take the lead

The Red Woman

45

Circe:
The Odyssey Sorceress

Many men have told my tale
They talk of pigs and nymphs
Of how I lauded over bays
And craggy island cliffs

They paint me as a heretic
And call my ways obscene
They say that I'm a haughty brat
A wicked, foul-mouthed queen

But I would ask you all to think
Of why I cast that spell
Why I turned those men to beasts
What creatures I repelled

It was not me who lashed out first
But I protect my own
Odysseus disturbed my peace
He did not sail alone

His men did not respect my home
They handled me like fruit
Poking at my bruising skin
And kicking me with boots

Was I so wrong to punish them
For making me their whore?
I could have done far worse you know
I'd murdered men before

Instead, I made them what they are
Those grubby, piggy beasts
And dined beside their captain dear
On pork and bacon feasts

Do not hate the sorceress
For slipping from the pyre
And making food of all those men
Who tried to light the fire

For I am not the villain now
And was no villain then
I was just a minor goddess
Cleaning out her den

I know it wounds your modern minds
To know I'm not that grand
A woman who struck back at life
With bloody, calloused hands

But I implore you please beware
Of history's dark lie
It's only told by conquerors
Not women who defy

Catherine Monvoisin:
The Parisian Poisoner

If people would remember me
I ask them to be kind
To recall I was a woman in a
Deadly kind of bind

Potions, tricks, and reading palms
Was something of a rage
And I decided early on
To shine from center stage

When Montespan first came to me
With heartbreak on her face
I knew what she would ask of me
My poisons left no trace

And though I took her offered gold
The plan, it fell apart
And she was left a mistress with
A broken, bleeding heart

I don't know why they came to think
That all the fault was mine
That each black mass or satanist
Was part of my design

I was one of countless girls
Who tried to make it rich
Who tried to walk the line between
A midwife and a witch

In the end, the king believed
That I was someone cruel
He tossed me on the flaming pyre
His words, they caught like fuel

And all throughout the Paris streets
Us poisoners did fall
To grasping hands of foolish men
Who thought girls should be small

I wonder with a smidge more time
Might we have offed them all
And been a town of women freed
From mankind's wrath and gall

But there's no way of knowing that
And so, I write this text
Dreaming from beyond the grave
That there will be no next

`

Tituba:
The Black Witch of Salem

It started on a frigid day
The Parris girl did writhe
She threw her hands into the air
A devotee at tithe

She kicked and howled and twisted fro
She bashed her head on earth
And in the storm she gnashed her teeth
Like Mary giving birth

I stared at her in silent fear
Unsure of what to do
A native slave inside her house
A stranger that was new

Once her seizing fit had stopped
I lifted up my head
Blinking in the dying light
She might have well been dead

Instead that girl did point at me
And venom on her tongue
She labeled me a wicked witch
And swore she'd see me hung

I told my story in the court
I vowed I'd tell no lie
But when they asked if I was bad
I pointed and replied

"T'wasn't me," I chose to say
"Though witch I well may be
T'was that Sarah Goody gal
Abigail told me"

And so, I dragged a wife or two
Into that foolsome play
Pretending that I was the beast
Those monster men would slay

I figured out their rotten trick
A lie would save your hide
But if you claimed your innocence
They'd say that you had lied

And so, I languished in a cell
Beside a motley lot
Wishing I possessed the nerve to
Speak true on the spot

That Parris man he beat me good
To make sure I held fast
He told me tales of dogs and birds
And witches with dark pasts

I know when people talk of me
They think of me as cruel
But there was little someone damned
Could do to win his duel

I pointed fingers, I hissed lies
I tried to flee from death
And I would do it all again
With every gasping breath

No soul within that wretched town
Was worthy of God's praise
Each and every one of them
Was evil in their ways

So maybe I'm an easy blame
The slave who turned her coat
I do not think the record books
Were right in what they wrote

For if they were, they'd look on me
With kinder eyes by far
And realize I was just a pawn
Who could not shed her scars

A woman's born to hold the world
Upon her bowing back
And bite her tongue until it bleeds
It's worse when she is black

I'm Tituba the witch of yore
I may have told some lies
But wouldn't you if you were me
I did not want to die

The Black Witch of Salem

53

Jezebel:
The Blasphemous Queen

When mankind wants to slur a girl
They slap her with my name
A way to call her horrible
But we are not the same

My only wrong was putting first
The gods I loved in youth
And lying to see Naboth stoned
But why was that uncouth?

My husband lusted after land
As kings were want to do
And Naboth held a healthy share
Was murder so taboo?

It wasn't right for Israelites
To turn their wrath on me
To throw me from a window
Without first heeding my plea

Dogs below they tore my skin
And cleaved it from the bone
Licking lips with bloody tongues as
Their owners seized my throne

If all I did was kill one man
And change what gods they praised
Then surely, I'm no wretch at all
And I'm no woman crazed

Ambition is a worthy trait
Unless you are a girl
Then you better play the ditzy
Peasant or the churl

If scheming with a sharpened wit
Is better than a blade
Then it applies to females too
For that's an even trade

And if those goons who murdered me
Are watching from below
I hope my namesakes aren't afraid
To give those pricks a show

Jeanne de Clisson:
The Lioness of Brittany

A noblewoman born and raised
Of healthy French-bred stock
I married rather young for love
He fast became my rock

Olivier was like all men
Ambition outstripped smarts
He was accused of treason and
His capture pierced my heart

I tried in vain to set him free
The crown did rage and scold
I could not break those locks, you see
The dungeons were patrolled

I did not stay to watch his head
Go bouncing 'cross stones
I had my sights on something grand
On toppling kings' thrones

I mounted up a mighty crew
And set sail on the seas
Painting every ship hull black
And doing as I pleased

My Revenge became my home
I tormented the coast
I wanted to make meals of rats
To watch king Phillip roast

My sons, they joined me at my side
We led a black-heart fleet
Until the fateful day we sank
Bereft at our defeat

We floated in the choppy waves
Adrift for many days
Guillaume withered to the bone
Until his eyes were glazed

Me and little Olivier
Were rescued by a friend
And taken to Morlaix to rest
To put my hate to end

And though the grief began to ebb
I would not leave the waves
I sailed for thirteen years gone by
Then shortly met my grave

Now I suppose the lesson here
Should be to live life slow
But why do that when you can strike
The men a hearty blow

A woman who lived life like me
Should pray and ask for grace
But I will not renounce my ways
My missteps, I embrace

Zheng Yi Sao:
The Chinese Pirate Queen

My life was not a shiny start
I grew up scrappy poor
I found work on a brothel ship
Enticed to play the whore

Before too long I caught the eye
Of Zheng, a captain lad
He asked me for my hand to hold
My finger he would clad

In little time the both of us
We built a mighty fleet
Sailing up and down the coast
The pirate world's elite

My husband drowned at sea and I
Was forced to lift my chin
To act like his loss never wracked
My sore and searing skin

I could have left the pirate world
To slink into the dark
Instead, I took the helm myself
And left my blazing mark

I gave no care to sin or stain
Zheng's son became my love
I made him king of all my fleet
My partner or thereof

For many years we reigned supreme
Ravaging the coasts
Stealing from West Indies Co.
And leaving them as ghosts

I might have sailed myself to death
And earned my neck a noose
But I could feel the changing tide
I deigned to sign a truce

In exchange I handed over
All that I had built
I settled into normal life
Without a shred of guilt

From gutter rat to pirate queen
I lived to tell the tale
And never once did I again
Lift sword nor flag nor sail

The Chinese Pirate Queen

Sadie the Goat:
The Queen of the Waterfront

I earned meself a silly name
But really it's the worst
I coined it from the penny mags
And streets that I traversed

A cutthroat and a gangster lass
Veins full of Irish blood
I ran with gangs inside New York
I was nay blooming bud

I traveled rivers on me ship
A pirate without waves
Freer than those girlish loons
No corset-wearing slave

Gallus Mag, she hated me
That six-foot bouncer dame
And so she cleaved a piece from me
A tale that's rather famed

I trawled the rivers with one ear
A little like Van Gogh
When pirate men mouthed back at me
I wiped their grins clean off

I'd shove them off a wooden plank
Which really soothed my soul
For they were mighty foul and mean
And questioned my control

I pocketed the wealth of men
All up and down those banks
And when they handed me their coin
A bullet was me thanks

I struck a truce with Gallus Mag
And she returned my ear
I wore it on a length of chain
A locket I kept near

And so, I lived a slapdash life
Pulling cons and tricks
Taking names and kicking arse
Until the final tick

Only when me time was up
Could I be heard to say
"I loved me life, sure and plain
I won't renounce my ways"

Shirley Pitts:
The Queen of Shoplifting

I never chose to be a thief
But rather it chose me
I had to steal to keep us fed
I could not pay a fee

The Forty Thieves, they taught me well
On how to use my looks
To steal from each department store
And falsify my books

I lined my pockets sure and true
Pinching from the wealthy
And though some people called me crazed
My mind was rather healthy

I never killed a single soul
I never hurt a girl
No, I was in it for the coin
In it for the whirl

So, when I died in ninety-two
The funeral was grand
They joked that I went shopping and
The devil lent his hand

For that's the kind of place for me
Forever made of stores
Lined with pretty dresses and
Uncountable sales floors

And if that type of life is found
In caverns deep as hell
Someone tell the devil please
I've come to ring his bell

Mary Fields:
Stagecoach Mary

I was not evil, I confess
Just rowdy with quick wit
I rode the deserts like a sea
A .38 and grit

Fighting off the cowboy gangs
And wolves and bandits both
Protecting mail from every ail
It was my solemn oath

I was not loved among the nuns
For speaking out of turn
But still I kept their mail for them
It lessened their concern

A woman with dark skin like mine
Had never held that spot
I wonder if that's why they like
To think of me as bought

Some stories make me out as bad
A crooked, gun-quick goon
I'm not sure why they think those tales
Are such a worthy tune

I was a stand-up, head-high gal
Who spoke just what she felt
And never turned her nose up
At the rotten cards God dealt

If always staying true to me
Is why they think I'm bad
Then every girl who ever lived
Is just as downright mad

Stagecoach Mary

Rose Dunn:
The Rose of the Cimarron

A rose among the Wild Bunch
Bill Tilghman once dubbed me
For running with the Doolin Gang
A rotten pack of fleas

George Newcomb was my lover dear
He worshipped at my feet
And all the gang defended me
From danger in the street

In Ingalls, we were cornered good
By marshals with their guns
As Georgie bled out in the lane
I took aim at those sons

Ammo slung across my chest
A Winchester in hand
I rushed to aid my lovely lad
To stamp them with my brand

I fired off a slew of rounds
They toppled with red necks
And I helped George escape the fight
To live to see what's next

I nursed the gang to better health
We hid and licked our pains
My brothers were headhunters then
Their victims fell like rain

For months we hid inside my home
I told them many tales
Of how I did not mesh with nuns
Of all my schooling fails

And then one day the brothers Dunn
They knocked upon my door
Shooting out the parlor lights and
Pockmarking the floor

I screamed and wailed and cursed those boys
No brothers were they now
What papers called a setup then
I greatly disavowed

I held George in my shaking arms
And tried to staunch the flow
But all that blood it covered me
Slick and wet like snow

His fingers slipped across my cheek
Then fell across his chest
I held him till his aching stopped
And clutched him to my breast

I sat there in the dying glow
Of all my many schemes
Knowing I was holding now
The remnants of my dreams

I hung my rifle on the wall
And bottled up my verve
Future lovers wondered how
I ever got the nerve

"A love like ours can move the sea
It shatters distant stars"
I smiled and then shook my head
"It leaves a slew of scars"

I settled into quiet life
I married once again
But never would I find a gang
That loved me like those men

A Wild Bunch they surely were
But they held dear their own
The loss of all those pretty souls
It cut me to the bone

Outlaws are not made of steel
They ache and scream and bleed
And underneath's a toothy beast
That has a desperate need

A need to make a name in lights
To make right every hurt
And us, we found that need fulfilled
In kicking hooves and dirt

Katherine Harony:
Big Nose Kate

A wild woman of the west
I blossomed and then died
But not before I wrote my name
On Tombstone's seedy hide

I loved my Doc despite our rows
I followed him through hell
I watched him shoot up rustler goons
He fought against death's knell

Consumption took him mighty fast
And what was I to do
I did not want to be the bride
Forever glum and blue

I honed my skills at pleasing men
And struck it rich in bed
While none could love me good as Doc
Lust kept my lips well fed

I never told of what I knew
Of shoot-outs at corrals
But I was known among the town
As every man's best gal

I gambled good as any king
A witty, outlaw lass
I lived a life chalk-full of warmth
Rough and loose and crass

If I could only live again
I'd do it just the same
Except I'd make my Darling Doc
Live long to see his fame

Eve:
The First Woman

I was the start of all this grief
The cause of all your pain
The reason that your stomach growls
With ambitions unexplained

You hunger for a world that's fair
But no fruit soothes your soul
And every place you lay your head
Your heart is but a hole

And just like me you look for men
Who balance out your ache
And try to make them understand
You fall for every snake

I know too well what it is like
To grovel on the ground
To walk on tiptoe everyday
Afraid to make a sound

I ate that apple not because
I thought it was not wrong
I took a bite because I knew
That I was mighty strong

Too long I catered to a man
A fragment of his side
A tool to make him happier
As shards of my heart died

Made to serve and hear his hurts
But he cared none for mine
A servant first and most of men
My tears were drunk like wine

Until the day a sweet-mouthed snake
Found me beneath my tree
And he said everything I felt
Just plain as it could be

He knew my thoughts, he shared my cries
He nestled round my neck
And though he could have killed me then
He gave my lips a peck

He gestured to that gleaming fruit
Glistening far above
And told me if I took a bite
I'd care far less for love

All my eager lust for life
Would be made clear as day
More answers than I ever gleaned
By folding hands to pray

I tore that fruit with greedy claws
Clean off its sagging twig
And brought it to my drooling lips
It tasted like a fig

That snake, he hissed against my ear
And coiled round my wrist
As Adam saw what I had done
He clenched his gentle fist

There's much he could have said or done
To goad me to a fight
Instead he took that fruit from me
And crying took a bite

When God arrived and scowled in hate
My Adam he declared
"It wasn't fair to keep us here
With knowledge left unshared"

And so, my God he shook his head
He glared right at that snake
And blinking back his scalding tears
His children he forsaked

"Do you both think this scaly beast
Can really know your heart?
It's I who made you from the dust
I thought I made you smart"

I did not weep as he announced
We had to leave that place
I clenched my teeth and bowed my head
I tried to hide my face

And so, it came that from one bite
My daughters came to be
Known as wicked women
That forever pay my fee

I'd change your future if I could
Erase your many pangs
And silence all the seething hate
Of men who gnash their fangs

But when I look at all you've done
You wretched and depraved
I am reminded all of you
Were born to misbehave

A little of me lingers there
Inside your gritted teeth
In the venom of your tongue
And in the veins beneath

And though my God would cast you out
I love you like that snake
Because you made a way from naught
And you refused to break

The world struck you and you struck back
With knives and fists and screams
And though you may have done it wrong
You tried to reach your dreams

Just like I reached for that fruit
You reached up to the stars
And finding skies were made for men
You wound up behind bars

In history books you'll always be
Foul villains best despised
If Khan can be a mighty king
Then you, my dears, are prized

Remember that when next they try
To stamp you with a curse
You're born of me and I'm afraid
Your mother's done far worse

The First Woman

www.ingramcontent.com/pod-product-compliance
Lightning Source LLC
Chambersburg PA
CBHW061503040426
42450CB00008B/1463